THE SIGNIFICANCE OF JESUS

THE
SIGNIFICANCE
OF JESUS

BY

W. R. MALTBY, D.D.

Burwash Memorial Lectures, 1928

TORONTO
VICTORIA COLLEGE PRESS
STUDENT CHRISTIAN MOVEMENT PRESS
58 BLOOMSBURY STREET, LONDON, W.C.1

To
E. H. M.

First published, May, 1929
Second Edition, July, 1929
Third Edition, November, 1929
Fourth Edition, October, 1931
Reprinted in "Religion and Life Books," September, 1934
Sixth Edition, May, 1936

PRINTED IN GREAT BRITAIN BY
THE GARDEN CITY PRESS LTD., LETCHWORTH, HERTS

INTRODUCTION

THE Committee in charge of the Burwash Memorial Lectureship congratulates itself on having secured as its third lecturer Rev. W. Russell Maltby, D.D.

Four of the addresses herein contained were given in the Chapel of Victoria University under the auspices of the Alumni of Emmanuel College, which is now the Theological College in Victoria University constituted of Union College (formerly Knox) and Victoria Faculty of Theology. It is needless to say these lectures awakened a profound interest. The Chapel was filled on all occasions. It would be difficult to over-estimate the religious values which Dr. Maltby brought to the Conference. In his visit to Canada Dr. Maltby did not confine himself to these lectures. He preached in the Convocation Hall of the University of Toronto, visited the societies of the Student Christian Association, and spoke at the prayer services of many of the Colleges. He also visited many University centres in Canada, and preached in many churches.

Henceforth many Canadians reading what Dr. Maltby writes, will do so with heightened interest as they recall the effective tones of his voice and the contagious influence of his religious faith.

R. P. BOWLES.

VICTORIA UNIVERSITY,
   IN THE UNIVERSITY OF TORONTO,
      October 5th, 1928.

NOTE

THE following Lectures were delivered in September last at the invitation of Chancellor Bowles and the Alumni of Emmanuel College, the Theological College of Victoria University, Toronto, to a very generous and indulgent audience, of whom I shall always retain grateful memories. Five Lectures were originally planned, of which the last would have been on "Jesus, the Saviour of Men." The occasion required only four Lectures and the Fifth was not written. This, however, was as it should be. If more was to be written on that high theme, it should be by a better hand than mine. I mention it here only lest anyone should think that I had joined the band of those who substitute the contemplation of a dead hero for the fellowship of a Living Lord. The road we travel in these Lectures does not end where they end. All the meanings we discover in the earthly life of Jesus deepen and converge to the mystery of His passion and shine out again in the glory of the Resurrection, but no doctrine of His Cross can dispense with the rich significance of His life.

W. R. M.

CONTENTS

Chapter I

JESUS YESTERDAY AND TO-DAY

THE seventy years of Biblical criticism through which we have passed must surely be reckoned among the major episodes in the history of the Christian Church. No other religion since the world began has undergone so fierce an intellectual ordeal, nor could any other have survived it. There are those who think that the whole trouble is due to the craft and subtlety of the devil, stirring up men in pride of knowledge to question the authority of the Church, or of the Bible, or both. But those who dissent from this strange notion and dare to think that even the *questioning* spirit is of God, must be willing to acknowledge that such times of unsettlement as we have lived through, have brought great distress to many minds, and chiefly to the non-combatants. For the protagonists on both sides had the exhilaration of combat and the occasional zest of victory, while the rank and file could do nothing but stand by and look on, doubtful at times if anything of the house of their faith would be left when the smoke of battle had cleared away. Half a dozen earthquakes or a considerable war would probably have involved less real suffering than the misery of doubt has occasioned to those whose heart and flesh cry out for the living God.

We may acknowledge all this, and still believe that something stronger than the hands of man or the subtlety of the devil is shaking the tabernacle of our faith. The mind of man, unless it is to be homeless and forlorn in a meaningless world, must build its own house, joining together the things it knows in some intelligible relation. The materials of its building are things known, things inferred, and things wished or feared, and we cannot be sure at every point what parts are permanent and what perishable. Nevertheless when we have built our house, we are in love with it, and we desire to rest from our labours and live in it. It is not only the believers who feel like this. Dr. Bertrand Russell having built his house, as he tells us, " on the firm foundation of unyielding despair," is just as resolute to defend it (though it seems a bleak site), as Mr. Gladstone was to defend his " impregnable rock of Holy Scripture." But God's wind and weather are always at work to search out the perishable elements in our structure, and time and again, when we longed only for finality and repose, we are required to rise and rebuild, or strengthen, or repair.

In the long controversy occasioned by modern Biblical criticism it is significant to notice how often the real issue has been mistaken on both sides. Orthodox apologists were often found fighting a rearguard action, evacuating by night what they defended by day. But it was not Christianity which they were defending at such times. In so far as they were contending for an infallible Book, the battle may be said to be definitely lost—and well lost, since an infallible book, whatever its conveniences, is an interdict on thinking, and therefore alien to the spirit of Christianity. Something better and richer than an infallible book is given to us both in the Old Testament and in the New.

In the Old Testament, as we now read it, we move in wider horizons than our fathers recognised. It is possible for us to watch there the patient ways of God with a strangely gifted race. We learn that revelation is not less truly God-given because it is not dictated but discovered. We can follow the conflict of true and false thoughts of God as they strove together in the minds of good men, and are now relieved of the hard necessity of thinking that God said all they thought He said. It is a great gain that we can see the prophets as men, and allow them to have second thoughts, and to correct and deepen their imperfect conceptions of God as experience taught them. Recovering the historical context of old prophetic words, we find them recharged with meaning, and in the wide sweep of moral law discover them to be relevant at once to their own time and to ours. But this newer way of reading the Old Testament presupposes something in the way of expert introduction—and some introducers, it must be admitted, do too much magnify their office—it requires some mental effort, some patience and a good deal of humility. And since many refuse to make this necessary contribution, they are apt to be left with a Bible vaguely suspect, and in the last push, uncertain everywhere.

The results of New Testament criticism have perhaps been less sensational, but they touch religion nearer to the heart. In the main they amount to a remarkable vindication of the genuineness and integrity of the documents.

Those of us who can remember the days when we clung firmly to the " four undisputed epistles " of St. Paul, and had to be content with arguments a little precarious for the dating of the synoptic Gospels *somewhere* in the first century, may well be thankful for the position as we find it to-day, when all the more important letters of St. Paul are sufficiently autographed, and the synoptic Gospels dated somewhere between the sixties and the eighties of the first century, with other documents of the like tenor reaching much further back.

The process by which the story of that unique life has been preserved to us is indeed utterly unlike anything which we should have expected, and if we still imagine that the more a process is human, the less it is divine, we shall find ourselves bewildered. We can watch those evangelists at work, collecting their materials, borrowing, eliminating, amplifying, in a free human way, with no paralysing thought that they were adding to the scriptures, or writing for all time. They have their limitations and their points of view. They give us fragments, and only fragments ; they are uncertain in their chronology and differ in the sequence of events : they leave strange gaps and are careless about many things which we should give all our treasure to know.

But one thing they did not do. Neither by their art nor by their artlessness did they hide Jesus. From the deliberate contemplation of their records, there has been given to us in our day a fresh disclosure of Jesus. The experts still have their synoptic problem and it may occupy them for some time to come ; and there are other questions of great moment on which scholars are not yet agreed. Nevertheless those who will, may see Jesus as no generation has seen Him since apostolic days.

There are many tokens that Jesus is again drawing the wondering eyes of men. One is to be found in the extraordinary output of books about Him—of which the more part are mercifully fallen asleep. Another token is to be found in the fact that the average man has begun to distinguish between Christ and Christianity, and to praise Christ at the expense of the religion which bears His name. All men speak well of Him now. This is good, though eager advocates should not make too much of it. It is a cheap thing to build the tombs of dead prophets. Once let it be understood that He whom we call Lord is safely buried nineteen centuries away, and there will be no lack of monuments. But in so far as this discrimination between Christ and His Church means that the significance of Jesus is challenging the attention of men in a new way, there is everything to be thankful for. And this is certainly true, both in Christian and in non-Christian countries. Someone describing the changing attitude of Indians toward the Christian message and Christian missionaries, traced three stages. First they said, Christianity is not *true*; then they said, Christianity is not *new*; now they say, Christianity is not *you*. Something like the same progress may be observed nearer home. Fragments of the teaching of Jesus are penetrating into unlikely quarters. Vexed with intractable social problems which will not solve *our* way, some have discovered that His way has never been tried, and some of His neglected sayings are found to be surprisingly relevant to our condition. Outside the bounds of the Christian Church, many are found ready to admit that He is the Light of the world, if there *is* a light of the world, and that He has the clue to the meaning of life, if there is a meaning. Starving for want of a little goodwill and peace with it, the modern world is more disposed to listen to

Him who spoke of it, possessed it and promised it to men. All this is to the good, and it may be the prelude to a movement toward God, deeper and stronger than anything as yet discernible among us. For if the Incarnation be the greatest thing done on earth, it must be a matter of infinite moment that that Incarnate Life should be presented to us as never before in its wholeness and simplicity, fresh, luminous, and inexhaustibly significant as we are finding it to be.

If we claim here that some significance of Jesus has been recovered for our day, that presumes that something had been lost, and it seems necessary to inquire how it came to be lost. To put our gains in a word, we have recovered the truth of the real humanity of our Lord. It is difficult to realise how largely this truth had been lost, even while it stood in the recited creeds, and called to men from the pages of the book they revered. Even now it is only beginning to enrich the experience and transform the outlook and conduct of Christian men. It came as a disturbing portent not a century ago, and the Church, not unnaturally, took up arms against it. For new truth never comes by way of mere addition to our stock, as though a new field were added to our farm.

Always the new truth shifts some old boundaries and this is why we usually go out to meet an unfamiliar truth with a gun in our hand. So this return of the Son of Man, if one may dare to call it so, came to disturb our imperfect theologies. The Church, of course, in its formal creeds has always asserted the true humanity as well as the deity of our Lord. But being more concerned to defend His divinity, which was always under the threat of attack, it fell into the way of affirming His divinity at the expense of His humanity, as though whatever was added to the one must be subtracted from the other. Accordingly those who showed unusual interest in the Man Christ Jesus came under suspicion of denying His divinity, and quite frequently the suspicion was justified. For this is the penalty which we must expect to pay for hesitating and intermittent loyalty to the truth, that others will neglect what we affirm in order to explore what we neglect. The Incarnation is indeed in the true sense a great mystery, and perhaps no one has really believed who has not first found it incredible. It has always been easier to surrender half the truth and to see Him either as a Man, even as the ideal Man, or else as a God who once for a little while wore the disguise of a human body.

B

The Church left the first alternative to the heretics, but fell into the second herself.

It is not too much to say that for centuries the Church was hardly in possession of the reality of our Lord's humanity, and therefore the synoptic Gospels lost the better part of their meaning. The Apostles' Creed taught men to say, *I believe in Jesus Christ His only Son our Lord, who was conceived by the Holy Ghost, born of the Virgin Mary, suffered under Pontius Pilate, Was crucified, dead and buried, He descended into Hell; The third day he rose again from the dead . . .* " passing straight, you observe, from the miraculous birth to the sacrificial death and victorious resurrection, without a word to record the significance of those thirty years, and especially those *three*. No doubt the Church had seized with a true instinct on the supreme moments of His revelation, but no modern student could be content to leave without a word of wonder and gratitude, those three crowded years of service, in which not one word or deed or gesture of Jesus fails to give us something that we could not afford to lose. Yet centuries of Christian literature followed the road indicated by the creeds, reproduced the same emphasis, and exhibited the same unconscious suppression.

The same scholars who grapple with the mighty arguments of St. Paul, and rise with him to the height of his theme, fall to the level of the commonplace when they come to the deeds of Christ, and are obliged to " spiritualise " them, to discover some " spiritual " analogy, before they can find interest in them or turn them to edification. By theological prepossessions of which they were only partly conscious, the Man Christ Jesus was hidden from them. Jesus was a divine mind in a human body. They were afraid to take seriously such words as those of St. Paul, that " though He was one in nature with God, He emptied Himself," or to follow the boldness of the writer to the Hebrews who returns again and again to the real humanity of our Lord, insisting that " it behoved Him to be made like His brethren in all respects," that " He Himself had experience of being tempted— tempted in all respects like ourselves, except for sin." Or still more daringly, " Having offered prayers and supplications with strong crying and tears and been heard because of His human piety, though He was a Son, yet He learned the lesson of obedience from His human experiences." Luther, indeed, broke out splendidly, " When I thus imagine Christ, then do I picture Him truly and properly. I grasp and have the true Christ, as He pictures Himself, and then I let go utterly all thoughts and speculations concerning the Divine Majesty and Glory, and hang and cling to the humanity of Christ ; then there is no fear there, but only friendliness and joy, and I learn thus through Him to know the Father."

But this was a voice crying in the wilderness. Christian interpreters thought of Jesus in the days of His flesh as equipped with all the resources of omniscience, and rejected the idea of any human limitations as though this were something dishonouring to Him. By so doing they removed from that Life almost all that makes human life what it is. They left no room for mental strife, for uncertainty, for ventures of faith, or indeed for faith at all, for surprise or disappointment, for suspense and frustration of plans. Temptation had no reality for Him, in any sense which we can understand. They did not *quite* do all this because the story was too strong and human for them, but the logic of their position pointed that way, and often they came near to bleaching all the colour and the wonder out of the one Perfect Life.

The story of the Temptation in the Wilderness is a crucial instance. A modern student finds in the account of the Temptation a clue to the whole ministry of Jesus and one of the most moving pieces of autobiography that literature affords. But none of the older commentaries has anything to say that is worth consulting on that episode. They did not apprehend its meaning and it simply did not interest them. They make such comment as they can, for it is the business of a commentator to comment, and apparently it is against the rules for him to say simply, " I do not understand this." We are told that the devil appeared " probably in a human form ": that our Lord " dispersed the assaults of the adversary like smoke." " We have here," says Matthew Henry, " the story of a famous duel, fought hand to hand between Michael and the dragon, . . . and our Lord comes off a Conqueror, and so secures not only comfort but conquest at last to all his faithful followers." For such expositors, the Temptation falls to the level of a sham fight between an omniscient God and a not very subtle devil, and as this view leaves little to expound, they hasten on to edification. They draw improving lessons from the passage, as for instance, the desirability of being able to answer the temptations of Satan in the words of scripture ; the wickedness of the devil in not finishing his quotations ; the virtue of fasting, in that our Lord " dieted for the combat, as wrestlers who are temperate in all things, but Christ beyond any other, for He fasted forty days and forty nights," a lesson which does not prevent the same expositor from pointing out that the fasting and consequent hunger left our Lord peculiarly exposed to temptation. How obvious it is that none of these useful lessons are derived from the story of the Temptation but are brought to it! It is pathetic that men intellectually so greatly endowed and spiritually of such insight and sympathy should have visited that desert scene blindfold and left nothing behind but a litter of tracts.

Dr. Sanday said that there was nothing more authentic in the Gospels than the account of the Temptation. Turn and look at it again. If we allow the Gospels to speak for themselves we must regard the Baptism of Jesus as an event which meant everything to Him. We do not know what went before, in those days when He must have known Himself different from other men—what strange surmisings, momentary intimations, sudden glimpses, what questions, and answers following. But in that hour of the Baptism, after whatever preliminary preparation, He knew Himself the Beloved Son of the Father and the Anointed of God. The same voice which announced His unique relation to God gave Him to the service and redemption of men. The tension of spirit which inevitably followed from such an experience is surely reflected in those later words which He addressed to His disciples when He asked them if they were able to be baptised with the baptism which He Himself had experienced. It drove Him into solitude and the desert, there to think out His supreme and awful task, to ponder what was to be done, or, where that was hidden, what was not to be done.

The account of what happened there must have come from Himself, and in telling it He showed to His friends the inmost secret of His heart. As a treasure is put in a casket that it may be preserved, so the story of those weeks of mental strife is cast in a kind of symbolism, that it might be remembered through days when it could not be understood, for the benefit of the days when it could. The truth is half-hidden that we may search for it the more, but when we have searched, surely it is plain that here is the record of long days of sifting thought, of patient disentangling of confused issues, of resolute discrimination between the best and the good which is the enemy of the best—all in a region unvisited by man, undreamed of by any of His contemporaries. As told to us, there were three temptations coming in orderly succession, but it was Jesus who reduced those weeks of strenuous thought to this simplicity. Temptations of the deeper kind do not "in the onset come" thus arranged and simplified, and it needed all the patience and utter sincerity of Jesus Himself to control that chaos of possible courses, all speaking at once, to force each to declare itself and be known for what it was.

He was conscious of supernormal power entrusted to Him and the significant thing is that it brought to Him first the apprehension of its dangers and a rigorous scrutiny of the right and wrong ways of using it ; and for Jesus this meant a scrutiny of God's way of using power, for the Son could do nothing but what He saw the Father doing.

He might have turned stones into bread— for Himself in His hunger, and therefore afterwards for others too. He knew what hunger was, and does anyone suppose that that compassionate heart was easily reconciled to the hunger of men and women. He refused, seeing what it meant. Later, upon a great occasion He made the venture. According to all four Gospels, He fed the multitudes miraculously. A right response was within their power, but they did not so respond, and a few days later He was obliged to tell them that they were dishonoured, for they followed Him for what they could get. Whether we accept the miracle or explain it away, the lesson remains, for we can see it in the situation. He gave men healing and He could surely have given them nothing so unexceptionable. But in a very little while, His message and His mission were in danger of being drowned in the only kind of miracle they cared about. Frantic crowds were fighting to get near Him in order to be healed. They would drive Him to the dilemma either to heal no one or to do nothing but heal. They left Him nothing but a mere knife edge to walk upon, but He found the way, and the principle underlying all His action is the principle of that choice in the wilderness, men were to be won, not *bought*, not even with bread, not even with health.

In the second temptation,[1] He was offered the kingdoms of the world on condition of some

---

[1] I follow St. Luke's order. Luke iv, 5.

act of homage to the power that ruled them. The temptation was much more subtle and difficult than some interpretations would lead us to suppose, for there is a place even for force in God's scheme of things. It was within His power "to break oppression" and "rule in equity," and He knew that the story of oppression is more pitiful than even the records of hunger. But He would not fight the world with its own weapons. He refused the kingdom of the second-best, the kingdom of this world, because men were to be won, not coerced even by a beneficent omnipotence. Again, in the third temptation, He refused to overawe men, to give them the sign from Heaven, the overwhelming proof for which they asked. He would not remove the option of faith, though He knew how doubt can harry us and mystery pierce.

It is said that the devil departed from Him for a season, for His choice was made and it was final, but how often and in what subtle forms were the same temptations pressed upon Him by friends and foes alike. The temptations were not those which come to a base or an ambitious or a presumptuous nature. They found Him on the side where He was most vulnerable—on the side of His compassion.

Food so hard to find, justice so hard to come by, God so hard to know—it was the woes of the world which called to that mighty heart and He found it hard to withhold. He left hunger and oppression and doubt in the world, though He armed all His followers against them. They were not to be abolished by the mere fiat of power. Every stage in this progressive refusal of the second-best was an act of reverence toward the human personality, a determination to leave the bounds of moral freedom where God had placed them, and a deep consent to the patient ways of God, startling to us who are impatient of God's patience and resentful of the inexorableness of His love.

But with this clue in our hands, is it too much to say that the whole course of the Gospel records acquires a new unity and a most moving significance? The miracles of Jesus used to be regarded as one of the chief evidences of Christianity, but when the attack shifted, they became one of its difficulties. Even now, some apologists think their task would be simplified if this supernormal element could be eliminated. No solution will be found, I think, in that direction. The tide already is ebbing in that creek and no boat will float long in those waters. But however that may be, it is certainly a mistake to imagine that the question is one about miracles in general. It is *these* miracles with which we are concerned, and if we intend to deal with the data provided, we shall have to answer two questions, Why Jesus worked any miracles, and Why He did not work more. For on the records the second is as much a problem as the first. Jesus, we may say, worked miracles because men must see that God is Master in His own world, that our limitations are not His bounds, nor even ultimately *our* bounds.

But the practice of Jesus also shows us that when miracles no longer opened the heavens, but only closed men the more effectually in the prison of sense, when they could not be made sacramental, then He avoided the occasions of them. If they were not received as an outward and visible sign of a spiritual Presence and an infinite kindness, they were not blessings, but bribes. They did not show God; they hid Him. When the darkness fell on that first Sabbath in Capernaum, Jesus, we are told, was going from one to another of the sick folk and healing them. It must have seemed to those who were there that the kingdom of Heaven had already come. By the morning fresh patients were ready for Him. But who among the disciples was capable of inventing what follows ? He was missing in the morning, and when His friends found Him, to bring Him back, He surprised them by turning His back upon His opportunities. He gave the word to go on to another place " that we may preach the Gospel there also." No one but Himself understood that He was maintaining the proportion of His life work, setting His mighty works in the context of His whole message, and rescuing His mission from the crowds which neither understood it nor cared for it. When a village showed hostility His most intimate disciples thought a little fire from heaven would be a very salutary lesson. They did not know what spirit they were of, still less did they know their Master's spirit, and it must often have seemed to them as if He kept all the hardships for His friends and spared only His enemies. Are there any words of Jesus more moving, more haunting, more profound than those words to Peter—Peter with the sword in his hand, bloody and ineffectual—" Do you not know that if it were to be done that way, I could now ask my heavenly Father and He would send me twelve legions of angels." Whatever may be meant by twelve legions of angels the purport is clear, that at a word He could free Himself if He would—and they were binding His wrists at that moment. Peter, and others broken-hearted like him, could only groan and ask within themselves why He did not call for the angels rather than permit this horrible thing to go on. If we can answer that question aright, we have a light to lighten the whole riddle of human history.

Right to the very end, and never more strikingly than in the difficult accounts of the Resurrection appearances, this unique bestowing and refraining confronts us. These gifts that cease when they would have become bribes, this power that stops short of coercion, these signs that persuade but never overwhelm, are the signature of Jesus on all His recorded deeds. The underlying principle is clear and intelligible now, though utterly uncomprehended then. He respected as no other has done the sanctity of the human personality, and He died rather than invade it, as He died in order to win it for God. " Behold I stand at the door and knock "—that is His word. It is not there that others are content to stand. Kings and captains have battered the door down. Priests have claimed right of

entry. Parents, stopped at that door, have dis-
owned their children. Only the Son of Man,
following the way of the Father, refused to do
us any violence, and had patience and humility to stand at the door and knock.

We can hardly help asking, even if we cannot hope for an answer, what would have been
the history of the Christian religion if the
Church had followed where its Master began,
if it had seen Him standing guard over the
sanctity of the human will, even when that
will refused Him. And still wider questions
press upon the mind.

I do not think that anyone can study Jesus
as He showed Himself among men without
marvelling at His inexhaustible significance.
There is not one of our modern problems, individual or social, to which He is not relevant.
Having once seen Him, how could His followers ever turn their eyes from Him, or look for
the glory of God anywhere else but in the
human face of Jesus Christ ? Yet they did.

" Even Athanasius," says Gwatkin, " dis-
cussed Christ entirely as a theological Person,
never, I think, otherwise referring to incidents
of His life, and the worship of saints in later
times is clear proof that He was not then
seriously regarded as a man." " There is no

steeper descent in history," he says elsewhere, " than that which directly follows the apostolic age. We pass at once from writings unsurpassed in creative power to writings of marked intellectual poverty."[1] But when, after a period, the thinkers reappear, the startling feature is the change of subject. The centre of interest has shifted. Theology is being systematised and the structure of the Church is rising magnificently to the skies, but the stones do not seem to come from His quarry and it is hard to believe that the plans are of His drawing. If the significance of those three years had not somehow been obscured, the miracles could never have been regarded merely or chiefly as proofs of His divinity, or His divinity chiefly as giving efficacy to His death, or His death made necessary by considerations mainly juridical. His life would not have been treated as merely the preliminary to His death, because one must live before one can die. If they had lingered over His teaching and made their own His sense of proportion, they would have seen the significance of His ethics, and He would have kept the doctrine of salvation moral and saved it from becoming magical or merely legal. If they had pondered His reve-

[1] *The Knowledge of God*, ii, 77, 79.

lation of the Father, they would not have needed to piece together their conception of God with elements borrowed from the seats of arbitrary power or the doubtful ways of Courts of Law. If they had been mindful of His example of humility and His repeated and even startling warnings against ambition and the love of power—*Call no man Master, for one is your Master*—a Church Council would surely have stayed before they declared that " our Lord Jesus Christ when about to ascend into heaven, left priests to represent Him as rulers and judges."[1] If they had lived with His parables and *felt* His sympathy with all the common toil and daily work of men, they would not, even unconsciously, have raised higher the barrier between the sacred and the secular and left the common people imagining that God had little or no interest in the things on which they were obliged to spend the better part of their days. Dean Inge has said : " We cannot suppose that the forms which Christianity has so far assumed—Jewish-Christian Messianism, the paganised Christianity of Western Catholicism, the fossilised Christianity of the East, the disrupted and fissiparous Christianity of the North—are any better than caricatures of

---

[1] *Council of Trent*, Session 14.

what Christ meant His Church to be." Too fiercely said, perhaps, to be just : but with too much truth for easy denials.

And now in our own day, once again we are confronted with Jesus, and it remains to be seen what our response will be.

CHAPTER II

JESUS VALIDATING FAITH

FATHER MARTINDALE in *The Faith of the Roman Church* tells us with sufficient plainness what is the ground on which a Catholic's confidence is built. "The sentiments (of a Catholic) may account for his fervour in practising his Faith; they may assist him to hold it with a new conviction : but they are not at all his reasons for believing that the Church's dogmas are true, or her commands right. A Catholic considers that he has cogent reasons for holding that the Roman Church is guaranteed by God to teach him only what is true, and to command him only what is right. He has then but to discover what she teaches and commands, and will proceed to believe the dogma, and obey the command, not only when he has no feelings about the matter, but when his feelings may be in a perfect tumult of opposition. . . . He does not believe a dogma because he sees very clearly what it means, nor because he thinks it would be useful, were it true. . . . He will, in short, think his personal feelings quite unimportant, since he may have good ones, or wrong ones, or none."

Words like these seem to most of us to belong to an alien world, and indeed the writer warns us that we shall find it so. Remembering some things which the Roman Church has at times " taught " and " commanded " one wonders by what mental process a distinguished scholar can repeat the claim that the Roman Church is " guaranteed by God to teach only what is true and to command only what is right." Cogent reasons would indeed be needed for a proposition which is to sustain the whole weight of the Christian Faith by guaranteeing the infallibility of any Church which history has known, and thereby making all other reasons superfluous or perilous. When we search for these " cogent " reasons, do we find anything but another instance how weak reasons become strong if we want them enough? Honest minds would never have maintained such a position except under some strong compulsion, and the compulsion has been, in part at any rate, the human hunger for certainty about God. Protestant Christians are apt to undervalue the immense advantage of a wide

general consent to the truths of religion,
because they are aware of its dangers. Like
other good things, it has its danger, and because it is dangerous and threatens the
vitality of religion, God sees to it that this
consent is from time to time challenged and
broken. But the times of this broken consent
are difficult,—not so much for scholars who
have the zest of theological reconstruction
and the relish of discovering one another's
infirmities, but for ordinary people, who, if
they want religion at all, want it to live by,
and not merely to think about. They look
for reinforcement where they are suffering
defeat, for the support of the divine Com-
panionship, and the sense of some great end,
which, even when dimly apprehended, re-
deems their lives from triviality and the curse
of littleness. The desire for such enlargement
of life finds its natural expression and its
deepest confirmation in prayer, which may be
the most significant thing that a man ever
does. Now the critical mood from which our
age cannot escape may easily disable us for
devotion. If one conducts an argument for
God, ever so successfully, the argument is not
a good immediate preparation for prayer.
We live in an atmosphere of question and de-

bate, and the questions often survive the answers, even when the answers have been good, and return to haunt the mind with vague uncertainties. There have been times in the past when those who sought God could find His temple not far away, and entering there, hear no discordant cries nor the echoes of debate, but only the testimony of many voices, made soft by distance, made sweet perhaps by death, all certifying that God was there. There one might leave off striving and surrender oneself to the encompassing Presence. If we were more childlike we might still find it true oftener than we do. But it is undeniable that for many it is not so. God seems hard to find. The questions of the mind being once raised cannot merely be put aside. Those who have once tasted intellectual freedom and know it to be the gift of God cannot take God on authority or assume Him for convenience sake. They cannot make the Christian affirmations, tremendous as they are, in the face of doubts which are not the doubts of pride or perversity, until they have found their way to some reasonable answer. It is no help to such perplexed minds to plead the authority of the Church or of the Bible, for the questions that rack the mind go back further and reach down deeper than the nature of the Church or the inspiration of the Bible. The doubt is rather as to the reality of a spiritual world and a personal God.

Of course, it is true that our fundamental difficulty with religion is to be honest enough to entertain it. This difficulty cannot be vicariously handled. Every man must deal with it himself. Many attempts have been made to construct a religion guaranteed to pass intact from father to son. But none of these attempts to gather a flock of unlosable sheep succeeds in the end. If we are to be religious we must have the chance of being irreligious. This is the will of God and not all the clergy and ministers of all denominations can make it otherwise, if they would. But this fundamental personal difficulty, inseparable from moral freedom, is complicated and aggravated if religion is presented to us confused by any self-contradiction or in any way inadequate to known facts. Once more the task is presented to this generation of showing the Christian faith in its essential beauty, wholeness and simplicity, and therefore with an inherent authority of its own. There is, I believe, already within reach a nobler, more reasonable, more comprehensive message than even our fathers knew,—and this not because we are wiser, or even more sincere than they, but because it is not for nothing that the Spirit of God has been at work upon the minds of men during these years of amazing research and fearless interrogation. That better message, however, has not been so articulated as to reach the average man, and if he asks only where or how to begin, he may have to wait long before he hears any satisfying answer.

If we reject the Catholic reply and refuse to answer uncertainty by authority we ought not to make the mistake of treating the craving for certainty as if it were something illicit or merely the weakness of uninstructed minds. Some of the learned do not seem to understand this hunger of the human spirit. They think it sufficient to base religion on a balance of probabilities and are satisfied if they emerge from the argument for God with the honours on His side,—or theirs. They do not see why we should not be content to live, for a few years at any rate, with God as a tenable hypothesis. Perhaps religion is for some men mainly a subject of investigation and its questions an exhilarating employment for the mind. But religion was not given to enable the wise and prudent to complete their intellectual scheme, and no religion is more intolerant than Christianity of provisional acceptance. Those whose heart and flesh cry out for the living God can no more be content with uncertainty about Him than they could be content to be uncertain whether their dearest friend was dead or alive. The contention of these pages is that if we look at Jesus some certainties stand clear. He is the Way.

It may be convenient first to summarise the argument which I am to submit.

1. Spiritual realities, if there are such things, as religion affirms, must be spiritually discerned. Whatever else this involves it means that there are moral conditions for spiritual vision.

2. The conditions of spiritual vision are not fulfilled in us, and it is not therefore surprising or mysterious that we discern these spiritual realities dimly and doubtfully.

3. But the conditions were fulfilled in Jesus, and His testimony, if it is accessible to us, is valid evidence of the reality of the spiritual world, and a real starting point for a personal faith, a real beginning of personal communion with God.

1. There are moral conditions for spiritual vision. This is not a dogma to be accepted on authority. If it is not self-evident, it needs only a little honest attention for anyone to see it to be true. We know, for instance, that in the appreciation of beauty something more spiritual, shall we say, is required than mere keenness of sight. A hawk may see a landscape better than I, but it cannot see what I see. I can see a sunset, but I cannot see what Turner saw,—although Turner can teach me to see better. It is obviously the same with moral excellence of any kind. Some men simply do not know what honour means. Self-centred people are not usually conscious of their selfishness, and when they attain to any degree of proficiency in their self-regarding habit, do not know love when they see it. The classical instance is the elder son in the parable, who full of his own behaviour looks round upon a home and sees nothing but rivals who come off better than himself. Even with an elementary virtue like honesty the same rule holds. The men who appropriate other people's money and are found out, almost always think themselves ill-used and blame everyone except themselves. " The blindness which is induced by all deliberate

injury to our moral nature, and which thickens its film as the habit grows, is one of the most appalling expressions of the justice of God. Moral evil is the only thing in His creation of which it is decreed, that the more we are familiar with it, the less shall we know of it. The mind that is rich in holiness and the humanities appreciates every temptation, computes the force of every passion, and discerns the degradation of every vice, with a precision and clearness unknown to the adept in wrong."[1] It is the great saints who were nearest to holiness who have given us the language of penitence as well as the language of aspiration. The sum of it all is that if we do despite to goodness or beauty or truth, after a time we cannot distinguish them. And the converse is stated once for all in the words of our Lord, *Blessed are the pure in heart for they shall see God.*

If we are inclined to pass this principle of the moral world as a commonplace, we should remember that it had a great place in the teaching of Jesus and a great place in His mind. Each one of the Beatitudes asserts that there is a spiritual world which is our true home, where alone our blessedness is to be found,

[1] Martineau, *Endeavours after the Christian Life* p.155.

and that we do not enter it because we do not *see* it ; and we do not see it because we violate the conditions of discernment. If we knew ourselves poor and famished for want of communion with God, if we had more divine discontent, if we cared for righteousness as we care for food and drink, then we should find the kingdom of God and His righteousness. We do not find it, Jesus tells us, because we do not want it very much. If we were single-minded in our search for truth or God, we should find. The lamp of the body is the eye, and the soul, too, has its organ of vision. But the spiritual eye is hurt and injured, otherwise we should be " full of light." It seems as though our blindness amid light so wonderful and satisfying, amazed and wounded Him.

Throughout the Gospels there is a continual emphasis on sincerity as though insincerity with the blindness which follows it were the one thing He feared for men. But sincerity, with Jesus, meant something much rarer and more fundamental than the thing we mean when we hand out certificates of " absolute sincerity " so freely to one another. It was integrity, in the more primitive sense of the word, truth in the inward parts, which He desired. The hypocrites whom He denounced in such terrible earnest were themselves in earnest about their religion. They were what to-day we should call " sincere " ; for the hypocrite may deceive others for a time, but himself all the time. It was this religious unreality always sinking below the conscious threshold, and never so mischievous as when it was unconscious, which disabled men from discerning the presence and the purpose of God. Jesus had mercy and hope for all, but if there were any who seemed past saving they were those who would follow Him about, arguing against the light, would thumb and finger each fresh deed of loveliness until its purity ceased to rebuke them and its kindness lost all power to persuade. The pure in heart *do* see God,—and they see sin ; the impure, the insincere, see neither the one nor the other.

2. From all this we draw two inferences. The first concerns ourselves. We discern spiritual realities but we discern them dimly and perhaps unconvincingly, because with us the organ of vision is partially disabled. This is not a dismal truth. On the contrary there is great comfort in it. For the dimness is for many people undeniable and it is far better that they should believe that it is because

they see badly than because there is nothing to see. One of the familiar hymns describes humanity as " bruised and mangled by the Fall." Whatever Adam had or had not to do with it, the line may be a quite sober description of our spiritual disability. They say that the sense of sin has departed from our generation ; yet who can stay for long in the light that streams from the life of Jesus without finding a thousand reasons why we are dark and confused where He was clear ? or who will deny that there is at least far more reason to mistrust our blindness than to mistrust His certainty ?

3. This brings us to our second inference and it concerns Jesus Himself. The conditions of clear spiritual vision are not fulfilled in us but they were fulfilled in Him. If anyone is at the stage when this seems too much to affirm, then let us say that the conditions were infinitely better fulfilled in Him than in us. I am not at this point assuming the full Christian affirmations as to the Person of Christ, not from any unwillingness to make them, but because we are not yet at that point of the road. Indeed those affirmations never ought to be *assumed*. They must bear themselves in upon the mind and shine in

their own light. But no one can give himself
to the study of the recorded words of Jesus
and mark the many ways in which He returns
to this demand for sincerity, without coming
to one sure conclusion,—that here was One
who was Himself of the deepest sincerity,
and that the spiritual realities of which He
spoke were utterly clear to Him. The Beatitudes are fragments of His autobiography.
He told His friends how they might enter
into the encompassing kingdom of God and
what it was that kept them out of it. But His
words would have been ridiculous and insincere if He were not Himself within. He saw
that men did not know what to do with their
lives but it is just as certain that He knew
what to do with His own. He saw men anxious
and burdened often to the breaking point,
but His own heart was at peace, and humble-
minded folk found His words credible when
He cried, "Come unto Me all ye that labour
and are heavy laden and I will give you rest,"
bade them learn of Him, because His yoke
was easy and His burden light. He was con-
siderate in all kinds of ways for His disciples,
yet He set them a task which He knew would
cost some of them their lives and all of them
paid a price which the world would consider

dear. But He did not falter and He never apologised to them, for He knew that the hope which He had given them would never let them down and that the zest they had learned from Him would not fail them. The conclusion of the Sermon on the Mount both in Matthew and Luke is a parable of utter simplicity which affirms that if men will build their lives on His word, their building will endure. Otherwise it will not, for life will only " work " one way and that is His way. Let any one test the words of Jesus for this element of certainty and he will find it everywhere and in ways far too subtle for invention. He is not groping or guessing. He spoke what He knew.

The great religious teachers of the world have not been credulous people. They have not been content with second-hand contacts : sincerity with them meant a passion for reality. It is, to say the least of it, a very difficult hypothesis to maintain that the highest of them all (to put Him no higher than that) was most deceived precisely in those things of which He was most sure, and for which at last He gave His life. If our human nature, in its supreme example with crystal clearness of vision, has no power to distinguish between reality and illusion, it seems hardly worth while to pursue any moral question further, for in that case, the world is not a revelation but a nightmare. Unless therefore we are to maintain that there can be *no* experience, however clear and constant, which amounts to evidence for the interaction of objective spiritual realities and the apprehending mind, we must admit the testimony of Jesus to be extraordinarily relevant and cogent.

But the argument carries us much further.

There is no meaning in giving to Jesus the name of a great teacher unless we believe that He was in some sense master of His subject. What was the subject of the teaching of Jesus ? Not, I think, as is sometimes said, the kingdom of God. It was God Himself. The beginning and the end of all He has to say, is God. The whole of that harmonious and perfectly integrated life rested on a faith in God verified in the most intimate experience. If He is not to be heard about God, He has nothing to say to us.

It has often been said that Jesus never argues for the existence of God. This is true, for it was not necessary for those to whom He spoke. But this does not mean that He took God for granted or invited others to do so. His whole intention is to make a new place for God

D

in the thoughts of men, to bring home to them the fact that by leaving out God they have turned everything to falseness and vanity. His teaching is steadily concrete and keeps close to conduct, but always in order to set conduct in its true context, that is, in the presence of God, whose name is Father and whose purpose we can apprehend.

So He showed them that their prayers were false because they were not really addressed to God. Since they had no thought of being heard by God, they hoped at least to be over-heard by men, and carried their prayers to the market-place to sell them for what they would fetch in the credit of men. Their charity had become corrupt because they had forgotten God, and nothing would put it right except to return to Him. They were censorious of one another because they had forgotten that they themselves were under God's scrutiny. They were anxious about food and drink and about what was going to happen to them, but they would not be like this if they believed in God and the reality of God's care. He would have His disciples live shining lives but the shining is to be traceable to their religion so that outsiders will say " This is of God " and glorify their Father in heaven. He rebukes the panic of His disciples in a storm at sea, though to us it seems excusable to be afraid of drowning. But He traces their fear to its roots and asks why they are of such little faith, why they should imagine that a storm was nearer or stronger than God. Indeed He found the world full of Little-faiths and marvelled at their unbelief, until He met here and there some one of a better mind, and then He marvelled to discover him. The unbelief which Jesus rebuked was not aggressive denial, nor too persistent questioning. It was the dull un-perceiving mind settled in a hopeless mood, because it had ceased to see God. And the faith which He desired, did not mean the choking down of doubts, or believing what one does not understand, or being content with bad arguments because they are used on God's side. It was the awareness of a sincere mind to the presence and working of God in His own world.

His subject then was God, but not " some kind of God." The God He reveals is a personal God, and it was a revelation. It is here that the doubt pierces to-day. Only a personal God can matter for religion, yet it is a personal God who is hard to believe in, and the difficulty does not grow less.

The Psalmist could find the universe a little overwhelming.

" When I consider the heavens, the work of
      thy hands
    The moon and the stars which thou hast
      ordained
    What is man, that thou art mindful of
      him ?
    Or the son of man that thou visitest him ? "

But in our day the argument of our insignificance is far more formidable, and with many of the more gifted and imaginative minds threatens to become paralysing. Rigorous thinkers may assure us that it makes no difference to the truth of religion that the universe is now known to be incredibly vaster and older than we thought, so that we must write off six figures and reckon in nothing less than millions before we can even begin to count. But it makes a great deal of difference to our *feeling*, and adds immensely to the difficulty of belief in a personal God if instead of a world not too big to be cosy, we find ourselves in a vast wilderness of space and time where myriad other worlds blaze till they are burnt out, where the history of the human race is but a late and transitory episode in a pigmy planet, a mere atom among the crowding giants of space. Is this one little corn of wheat the only significant thing in this mountain of straw?

The difficulty is new in its intensity, but it is not of course a new difficulty. It has always been found difficult to reconcile greatness and kindness. With us greatness always seems to grow cold. A typical example may be found in the religious thought of India. The thinkers of India, with the pulses of the eternal in their blood, made a God out of vastness. They laboured to apprehend his greatness and refused every kind of limitation. They lifted him above all our distinctions. He was the All. He was neither good nor bad, neither true nor false, or, if you preferred to put it that way, he was both the good and the bad, both the false and the true. He was far too great to know or to care. He was the Unknown and the Unknowable. So they completed the circle until the Infinite touched zero again. But human nature unable to endure this frigid abstraction began again and out of the legendary figure of Krishna created an intermediate God not utterly inaccessible to the spirit of man.

If some kind of communion was thus made

possible, it was never free from the whisper
that it was all illusion. The Buddha knew of
no God and therefore in his sincerity spoke of
none. He found a Wheel instead. All races
have had their idea of an impersonal Fate
which governed the lives of men, a Fate which
sometimes seems to put on justice and has its
moments of pity, only to fade off again into
the impersonal and non-moral. Much of our
modern literature is haunted with unhappiness
because it sees the aspirations of mankind
continually defeated by some inexorable Force
which takes no account of good- or ill-desert,
and lifts up or treads down with majestic
indifference. The mechanistic philosophies of
our day believe that they can describe the
nature of this self-acting universe and find no
room for the God of religion. When the idea
of evolution began to prevail over the preju-
dices which it first encountered, religiously-
minded people used to seek anxiously for
breaks in the majestic sequences of cause and
effect which science was disclosing. They
looked for the places where there was no
traceable antecedent, so as to give God an
opportunity of keeping His hold upon the
world. But the breaks are difficult to establish
and at any rate are fewer and less decisive than

they were thought to be. And if we are driven back to the beginning and argue that the universe cannot have started itself, and must have a First Cause, the argument may be good, but a God so remote and non-moral has no value for the purposes of religion. Now therefore we have come to see that God must be everywhere or nowhere, and we no longer look for Him in the gaps which research has not yet explored, but in the filled spaces of the common life about us. This is good; nevertheless experience proves that for practical purposes a God " everywhere " may be very much the same as a God " nowhere." It is still a personal God that we need.

This question of a personal God is of course vital for Christianity, yet it is just at this point that many to-day sustain the worst assaults of doubt. They find it easier to see the " Wheel " than the Person ; to acknowledge Force than to recognise Purpose. The sun rises indifferently on the evil and the good ; the rain falls on the just and the unjust ; floods and plagues do not discriminate between useful and useless lives ; the sea that floats a lifeboat will carry a pirate and the stars in their courses sometimes fight for Sisera and confound Deborah. There are

1,500 million human beings on this little planet, of whom the greater part came into the world anyhow and live anyhow, caring for little else but food and drink and shelter. Does God really remember them all? Does He number the very hairs of their head? Has He some meaning for each one? If one of them is made to stumble, does He burn? May so small a creature cry, and be heard by the God who built the atom and flung out the stars? It is a tremendous affirmation. If any one can make it lightly, he must be innocent,— and therefore, God bless him! Yet it is the affirmation of the Christian religion.

Let me remind you, by way of clearing the ground for the fuller argument, that if there is no coercive proof of the existence of a personal God, there is no coercive proof to the contrary. This may easily be established. Physics to-day holds the floor in science and its speech is wonderful enough to keep all others silent. But some of the foremost men in physics are Christian believers, and this is not because they keep their religion and their science in separate compartments, which is more than ever impossible for first-class minds. Their physics left faith as an option. And again there are other men acquainted with the same facts who are not believers,—unbelief was an option. Neither theism nor atheism is forced upon us by any facts which science can investigate and the door is left open for other kinds of evidence. It is legitimate to hear the testimony of the saints. It is above all legitimate to listen to the evidence of Jesus.

It is of course beyond question that the whole ministry and teaching of Jesus bear witness to a personal God, continuously verified in a living experience which in depth and richness is wholly unique. He brought a new revelation and because it was new, He needed a new name for God. But He did not look for it in the courts of kings or search for a word to express majesty and power. He preferred for us the risks of intimacy rather than the chill of distance, and gave us the name " Father " which of itself invites to childlike and intimate relations. He encourages men to trust the analogy as far as it will go, assuring them that if they are childlike in their approach to God, they will find the divine response. He does not speak of " Fatherhood." If this was because there was no such word in Aramaic, we may still be thankful. But there is a deeper reason. In all His thinking He is actual and concrete.

Therefore He does not use abstract terms, like "love" and "fatherhood." He chooses the simplest dealing between father and son and asks "Which of you being a father, if his son ask bread, will he give him a stone?" And when he had given time for a man to say within himself, "No thank God! bad as I am, I am not as bad as that," He goes on, "How much more will your heavenly Father give good gifts to them that ask Him!" He told men to ask and it should be given, to seek and they would find, to knock and the door would be opened,—three ways of saying the same thing, and having said it, proceeded to say it again: "For every one that asketh receiveth, and he that seeketh findeth, and to him that knocketh, it shall be opened." This is significant enough, but the words are suddenly re-charged with meaning when we remember that the deepest and surest experiences of His own human life lay behind these words. He told men to do only what He had long done Himself, with those results. He promised men nothing which He had not already verified. He himself in hours more sacred than we can conceive, had entered into the inner chamber, shut the door and found the Father.

The three parables in the fifteenth chapter

of St. Luke's Gospel tell us that there is a
spiritual encompassing world, out of our sight,
which is concerned with the individual doings
of men, and that the recovery of one single
human being to God and to goodness is the
occasion of " joy in heaven." The parable
which we call the parable of the Prodigal Son
is unique among the parables of Jesus. Most
of the parables of Jesus are intended to light
up a particular situation or to point a special
truth, and we do them wrong if we press them
beyond their intention. But in this parable
there is a loving workmanship as if the story
had long been turned over in His mind. It is
in fact the story of God and His world as Jesus
saw it, and it affirms what we can only call
the passion of God for the souls of men.
Clutton Brock calls it the most beautiful story
in the world, and we find it in what Renan
called the most beautiful book in the world.
The son comes home because he is starving,—
nothing more creditable than that. But from
the moment he is seen returning, the whole
situation passes out of his hands. He stammers
his little speech, and breaks, and then has no
more to say, but sits dumb with pain and joy
and wonder before the revelation of what the
father's love really means. And still this is not

the climax,—not the kiss of reconciliation, nor the feast, nor the music, nor the dancing, nor the words, " This is my son." There is still another son, who has tried to live on good behaviour as his brother tried to live on bad, and he too has starved on that lean diet, but he is sullen and aggrieved and slanderous. Yet all that the Father says to him is, " Son, if you did but know it, all that is mine is thine." This father is God. Could any one with an open mind listen to such words from such lips and *not* say, " I too will arise and go to this Father."

see p 42

Such things ought not to be said unless they are true ; they ought not to be said unless they are *known* to be true, and Jesus who spoke the parable needed no reminder from us to give heed to what He said. This language speaks to every man in the tongue wherein he was born ; it borrows its appeal from the region most sacred to us all and addresses the deepest and most piteous needs of the heart. Millions of men have trusted such words as these and thought them verified. If all is illusion and these too confiding souls were deceived, we have to say that Jesus Himself was deeper in the illusion than any of us. Every man must decide for himself whether that is a possible hypothesis.

CHAPTER III

JESUS ·HUMANISING THEOLOGY

MAY I forestall, if I cannot appease, the critic, by acknowledging that I do not like the title which I have given to this lecture, but I do not know how to mend it. I should have preferred to speak of Jesus *rationalising* theology if the word meant, as it ought to mean, making things reasonable, and intelligible. But since it has been annexed by those who have no sense of spiritual values, who use it to explain away the soul of religion, and destroy in order that they may anatomise, the word is no longer serviceable for any purpose that I have in view.

We must all be aware that there is a modern demand that relegion, and the theology which attempts to give a coherent account of it, shall be reasonably and intelligibly offered to the mind. The demand is not new in the sense that it has never been made before. It would be nearer the truth to say that there was never a time when the demand was not heard, and there have never lacked some in the noble succession of apologists, who endeavoured to answer the intellectual difficulties of their own age, to show the greatness and consistency of the Christian Faith, and made it their aim to " justify the ways of God to men." But the demand for reasonableness in religion is new in its urgency and in the strength of feeling and conviction behind it. It is new also in that it comes from those who wish to believe rather than from those who wish no such thing.

The demand will not seem strange if we remember two things. On the one hand there has been an immense decline in the prestige of " authority " in nearly every region of thought and conduct. All authorities are now required to produce their credentials ; and since it is part of the notion of authority that it does not make mistakes or give wrong guidance, it is difficult to see what external authority is likely to survive the test of its own history.

On the other hand, while the realm of authority has shrunk, the territory occupied by the exploring and enquiring mind of man has been immensely extended. The achievements of Science during the last century have been extraordinarily impressive, and they have been achieved by the rigorous interrogation of facts, and frequently with a fearless but necessary disregard of authority. The faith which underlies all modern research is that the universe is intelligible, and each fresh advance is a confirmation of that belief. The world invites us to enquire into its secrets, and treats us handsomely when we come. Vast tracts formerly unknown have been reclaimed for our understanding and our use, and the pioneers of research are steadily annexing fresh continents. Even the simplest persons are expectant of new and revolutionary discoveries. The keys are in our hands; one by one the doors fly open; " No Paradise," it seems, " stands barred to entry."

All this reacts powerfully on the mind of our time. Indeed the change in our mental world is quite as significant as the change in our material environment. The credulous are still the majority among mankind but the majority is not quite so overwhelming, and they are credulous in a different direction. This is the day of Science. People who are contemptuous of the technical language of the theologian listen devoutly to the technical language of the radiologist though the latter is certainly not any more intelligible to them. Even a quack nowadays must pretend to explain, and must dress his quackery in the garb of science, if he would make sure of his reward. But when we come to the truths of religion, the case is different. Whoso would commend religion to men to-day, must reckon with a critical audience demanding that he be reasonable and we need not complain that it is so. It is possible to convince reasonable men that when they come to deal with spiritual realities, the method of study, the nature of the evidence and the conditions of verification will be different from those which were found valid in the examination of material things. But the demand for reasonableness will take no denial and it will not be possible to persuade men to believe in any mystery which merely confounds instead of enlightening the mind, and is not capable of *some* kind of verification. They will not and ought not to acquiesce in the irrational, or the magical, or the arbitrary in religion.

Now religions of authority do inevitably tend to shelter arbitrary elements. Authority is not required to give reasons for particular beliefs, but when the inevitable questions arise it is always under the temptation to offer bad reasons,—not only because it has always a final argument in reserve, but also because it speaks to an uncritical constituency where a docile assent has come to be regarded as a sign of grace and a virtue of sovereign efficacy. It may be argued that many vital truths have been preserved by authority, which would otherwise have been lost. Perhaps this is so, though it remains a " perhaps," because the true authority,—the witness of the truth to itself, has never been tried out. It is, however, simple matter of history that religions based on external authority have sheltered and sanctioned beliefs and practices, sometimes irrational, sometimes morally repugnant, quite alien to the spirit of the religion in which they were incorporated. The system having been once closed, there was no remedy. Evils or errors once included, must remain, although the free action of the human mind would have ejected them if it had not been inhibited. The result has been the more disastrous, because quite often these alien and unworthy elements have taken command, and subdued the nobler part to their colour.

The Athanasian creed is perhaps the instance that comes first to the mind. *"Whosoever will be saved: before all things it is necessary that he hold the Catholick Faith.*

E

Which Faith except every one do keep whole and undefiled: without doubt he shall perish everlastingly. And the Catholick Faith is this . . ." We may admire what follows as a courageous attempt to find language for sublime truths and unfathomable mystery. But to make it the gateway of salvation, and to require assent to a metaphysical statement of the Being of God,—a statement necessarily unintelligible to almost all, with the promise of salvation as the inducement to believe, and the threat of eternal damnation if one demurred,—was to sin grievously against the sublime reasonableness of our Lord.

Probably not many of us here are troubling ourselves about the Athanasian Creed, now nearly eleven hundred years old, but this is not the point. The Creed represents the teaching of the Church for centuries both before and after, yet it might have been challenged from almost any page of the Gospels. There is no sort of relation between the message of Jesus and the demands of the Athanasian Creed. It is neither His strait gate nor His easy yoke. It is the symbol of a system which substituted orthodoxy for faith, and a creed for a Person. Instead of a personal trust, charged with moral quality, it demanded an assent which,

with some, could only be a non-moral acqui-
escence, and with others, an immoral capitu-
lation. If men had been taught to say,
" Whosoever will be saved, it is *not* necessary
that he hold the Catholick Faith," they would
have been taught a truth, and a needful
truth, though of course a partial one. But the
Church could never have moved so far from
the mind of Christ and put a stone of stumbling
where our Lord had left an open door, unless it
had first made the Gospel records a palimpsest,
where the truth as it is in Jesus was barely
discernible beneath the overwritten speculations of men.

The Calvinistic theology may be cited as a
second instance.

No one need grudge to acknowledge his
debt to Calvinism. It was conceived by strong
and massive minds and it did not breed
weaklings. It had elements of truth and
strength of which we are rather sadly in need
to-day. But if we ask what account it gives
of the ways of God, we have to say that it uses
language which has no real meaning if it does
not describe an arbitrary God.

I suppose the hardiest surviving predes-
tinarian could hardly read out the several
paragraphs of *The Sum of Saving Knowledge*

with their terrible clarity and their iron precision, without apology and some attempt to temper their merciless logic. The Confession of Faith, full as it is of strong thinking on better themes, is less startling than *The Sum of Saving Knowledge* but it is sufficiently explicit.

" By the decree of God, for the manifestation of His glory, some men and angels are predestinated unto everlasting life, and others foreordained to everlasting death.

" These angels and men, thus predestinated and foreordained, are particularly and unchangeably designated ; and their number is so certain and definite that it cannot be either increased or diminished."

Or again,—" The rest of mankind, God was pleased, according to the unsearchable counsel of his own will, whereby he extendeth or withholdeth mercy as he pleaseth, for the glory of his sovereign power over his creatures, to pass by and to ordain them to dishonour and wrath for their sin, to the praise of his glorious justice."

Good men once heard such words and, because they were of humble heart, believed them, thinking it would be presumptuous to question what seemed to have been revealed. But when they were obliged to defend them, desperate as the argument is, it comes to no more than this, that these are the ways of God, and being the ways of God, they cannot be arbitrary, but must be altogether good and right. We remember how this doctrine of election and reprobation cut across the evangelical revival of the eighteenth century and would have paralysed it at its beginning if it had not been fought and routed. John Wesley fought it with sermons, appeals and addresses. Charles Wesley fought it with scalding rhymes :

> " The righteous God consigned
>   Them over to their doom
> And sent the Saviour of mankind
>   To damn them from the womb;
> To damn for falling short
>   Of what they could not do
> For not believing the report
>   Of that which was not true."

But the real answer was the evangelical revival itself. The debate in anything like its old form, is ended, but the mischief did not begin with Calvinism nor did it end with it. The question concerned is nothing less than the character of God, and the God who was thus presented to men was not the God and Father of our Lord Jesus Christ. When Jesus spoke of God, He pointed men to the home and told them to watch the ways of human love at its best and highest, remembering only that His love is " how much more " than ours at its best. They looked where He pointed, and learned much, but they hurried away too soon, and betook themselves to the courts of kings, to watch the ways of sovereignty, and learn greatness from the great. They should have stayed longer where He pointed, and laid to heart the lesson He taught, that while human love is of the same nature as God's love, human greatness is not at all like God's greatness but altogether another thing.

If we were to come to later instances, we should be on more controversial ground. One might recall the arguments by which good men defended their terrible doctrines of eternal punishment. Sin, they said, deserved an infinite punishment because it had an infinite guilt, and it had an infinite guilt because it offended against an infinite Being. It was the doctrine of *lèse-majesté* imported into the relations between God and man. Yet Jesus speaks quite differently and teaches us, in words that ring with passion, that the darkest offences are those which are committed against the weak and the defenceless.[1] Or, if one may venture on still more delicate ground, where controversy is still acute, one might ask the meaning of that strange distinction, which nowadays is to carry such a weight of consequence, between covenanted grace and uncovenanted mercies, as though *that* was secure, while *these* were precarious, and as though God kept His Covenant, and sometimes out of compassion, did a little more.

It is not my wish to raise controversial issues, nor do I care to argue that the instances I have offered are the best that could be chosen. It is enough if we see that when the mind of our time, instinctively seeking to integrate all it knows, challenges the arbitrary in religion and demands reasonableness, we cannot reply that the challenge is gratuitous. For the history of these arbitrary intrusions into the Christian Faith has been long and disastrous. They have entangled Christian apologists in the defence of what was indefensible ; they have alienated many noble and truth-seeking natures and they have left a certain deposit in the minds of masses of ordinary people which makes them think

[1] Mark ix, 42.

that religion is beyond their understanding and little concerned with their life. The demand then for a reasonable theology is not wholly perverse or groundless. Our Lord would I think Himself endorse it, and in the meeting of it He is Himself of supreme significance. No man can listen long to the Jesus of the Gospels and complain that He is obscure or arbitrary or unintelligible. On the contrary we find that our demand for reasonableness is turned back upon ourselves and that our difficulty is not with Him but with ourselves.

To begin with, nothing is more certain than that religion was all luminous for Jesus Himself. He lived and moved and had His being among spiritual realities which were as clear to Him as towers and trees are to us. And those same realities were dim and doubtful to us, not because they were hard to see, but because we were blind, and blind because we were perverse. He spoke of the things of God in language of a unique simplicity, and this simplicity was the outward sign of an inward clarity. There are passages in His teaching, of inexhaustible significance, which yet contain not a single word which would be unintelligible to a child. He rescued religion from the hands of the experts,—blind leaders of the blind as they then were,—and restored it to the apprehension of the common people. He watched with joy while quite simple people entered into His secret, and broke into thanksgiving that it should be so. " I thank Thee O Father, Lord of Heaven and earth, that thou hast hidden these things from the wise and prudent, and revealed them unto babes."[1] He told the twelve that they must get rid of their adult sophistication and the blinding habit of self-seeking, and go back to the simplicity of children, and then they would enter the realm where He dwelt and see what He saw.[2] When the crowd wondered at His teaching because He taught with authority and not as the scribes,[3] they did not mean that He was dogmatic or required them to believe what He said, merely because He said it. They meant that He spoke as one who knew what He was speaking about. He said that the mind was made for the truth as the soil for the seed,[4] and assumed that we have a capacity for discerning the truth when it is presented to us if we are open-minded and lovers of the truth. He argues, when necessary, but He does not cumber the truth with argument when argu-

---

[1] Luke x, 21.   [2] Matt. xviii, 3.
[3] Mark i, 22.   [4] Mark iv, 26.

ment is not needed, knowing when honest minds had already seen " and believed," and dishonest minds had shut the door.

Faith occupies a great place in the mind of Jesus but it is questionable whether it is not misleading to speak as some do of His continual demand for faith. For He knew that to demand faith is to set a man labouring with his own mind, and perhaps tampering with his intellectual integrity in the effort to believe, instead of looking at the object of faith. But it is true that He was always looking for faith, and recognised it for what it was when we should have called it by quite other names. Jesus sees faith where we should have seen superstition,[1] or perseverance in the face of discouragement,[2] or straightforward common sense[3] or even a piece of audacity.[4] But whenever a man, having a glimpse of the better thing, started up to meet it, Jesus recognised this as faith and honoured it accordingly. Unbelief on the other hand, as He saw it, was nearly always a dull thing ; it is slow and stupid, but the stupidity has moral roots. He welcomed and almost required alertness of mind and rebuked the Twelve with

[1] Mark v, 34. [2] Matt. xv, 28.
[3] Luke vii, 9. [4] Mark ii, 5.

some severity simply because they were being, as we should say, rather wooden. But they were wooden because competing interests and rival loyalties were confusing their mental processes and preventing them from apprehending His meaning.

Many of our Lord's parables are simply an appeal to act as sensibly in the concerns of the soul as we do in the things of the body. Worldly men, He said, manage their business better than the saints.[1] We are told stories of " ten virgins " and five of them were " sensible " and five were " stupid,"—equipped with lamps that would not burn; we hear of houses built on shifting sand; of towers begun without reckoning the cost and left unfinished as monuments of somebody's folly; of kings who go to war without reckoning the enemy's forces; of a householder lamenting that he had not known at what hour of the night the burglar was coming, otherwise he would have sat up and not allowed him in. The wicked and slothful servant is judged out of his own mouth and convicted on his own evidence, and the rich man planning the building of bigger barns hears a voice saying, " Thou fool." The folly of it all!

[1] Luke xvi, 8.

With Jesus, there is no mystery merely for mystery's sake. Nothing is hidden, but in order that it may be revealed,[1]—so He tells us, giving us the freedom of every realm of knowledge. Nothing was wanted but eyes, and this was His complaint against men, that " seeing they see not and hearing they hear not, neither do they understand." Light was come into the world, but in some regions men prefer darkness to light. " He that hath ears to hear," He reiterated, " let him hear," which is to say, " God has given you minds ; use them ! "

When we watch the stages of the conflict between Jesus and the religious authorities of His time, we see the moral incompatibles which made the collision inevitable. But of the various aspects of that conflict, it is not the least important that it was a conflict between sense and nonsense in religion. When Jesus said, " The Sabbath was made for man, not man for the Sabbath," the thing which He affirmed was heavenly wisdom, the thing which He denied was lunacy, but it was lunacy for which God was made responsible. When men were punctilious in tithing mint and anise and cummin, and indifferent to justice

[1] Mark iv, 22.

and love, as though religion were concerned
with those trifles but not concerned with
moral realities, they made God Himself irrational. When trivialities were elevated above
first principles, and rites observed the more
rigorously as all moral significance went out
of them, when the honour of God was being
set in opposition to the succour of men, it
was evident that all sense of proportion was
being lost in a world of names and shadows.

The perfect sanity and sense of proportion
which were pre-eminent in Jesus have often
been acknowledged. But His interpreters
have been more slow to recognise a kindred
quality which I suppose we must call humour.
It is now conceded more freely than once it
was, thanks largely to Dr. Glover, but even
yet too timidly and with inadequate appreciation of its importance. For, indeed, the matter
is of very great importance. Many people do
not understand the office of serious humour
and continually confound reverence with
solemnity, or with a gravity which is, as
Bacon says, "lumpish and almost leaden."
One writer in a book on our Lord's teaching,
full of excellent matter, says of Him : " His
voice and utterance were, in general, of a calm
solemnity, without vehemence and without

agitation. Only this is consistent with His language and His attitude; for He *sat* in preaching, whether in the synagogue, or on the mount, or in the boat when speaking to the people on the shore." If sitting and solemnity must go together one cannot help wishing that some authors would write standing. One would have said that not until the words of Jesus had been heavily steam-rollered could their infinite variety be flattened to such a description. Story and argument, epigram, and paradox, humour and irony, homely analogies and pictures from the grotesque, piercing questions, daring transitions, breath-less pauses and then—that sudden leap to the mark—how could it be supposed that all this was delivered in a level voice or with a fixed countenance, or that Jesus Himself did not feel the zest of such speech or failed to give it the proper accompaniment of gesture and expression.

This notion that nothing but a fixed gravity of expression befits our Lord was never de-rived from a study of His words. It belongs to a misconception of the religious life which has, as I believe, very mischievous conse-quences. Cardinal Newman expounds it more explicitly in his sermon on Religious Emotion.

" That perfect state of mind, at which we must aim, and which the Holy Spirit imparts, is a deliberate preference of God's service to everything else, a determined resolution to give up all for Him, and a love for Him, not tumultuous and passionate, but such a love as a child bears towards his parents, calm, full, reverent, contemplative, obedient. Here, however, it may be objected, that this is not always possible ; that we cannot help feeling emotion at times ; that even to take the case of parents and children, a man is at certain times thrown out of that quiet affection which he bears towards his father and mother, and is agitated by various feelings ; again that zeal, for instance, though a Christian virtue, is almost inseparable from ardour and passion. To this I reply, that I am not describing the state of mind to which any of us has *attained*, when I say it is altogether calm and meditative, but that which is the *perfect* state, that which we should aim at . . . . At all times the religious principle, viewed by itself, is calm, sober and deliberate." Newman proceeds to illustrate from Scripture. Agar is praised for his quietness, Joshua for his composure, Job for his calm resignation, while St. Paul is excused for his " greater fervency, because he was in more distressing circumstances " although that fervency, we are warned, did not give to his avowal any " more acceptableness in God's sight." If anything were needed to convince us that something was wrong with the argument, it would be the curious and inconsequent scriptural illustrations adduced in confirmation. We read the whole sermon with alternating assent and dissent, but in the end, it is plain that Newman is expounding a traditional conception of the religious man, scrupulous, pallid and subdued, which he had never seriously tested by any part of the Bible, least of all by an impartial study of the Gospels.

It is strange that religion and the sense of humour should have fallen out so often,—always to the degradation of humour and the impoverishment of religion. If we turn over books of piety such as were read fifty years ago, we find ourselves admiring the earnestness of their intention, but we miss the antiseptic of humour. Their disciples must stand always at attention. The tension is never relaxed. There is an almost ruthless concentration upon edification and it finds expression in a language which labours with the strain of conscious effort. They do not say they are glad : they say that they are " enabled to rejoice." They do not work : they are " permitted to labour." They do not attend a meeting : they are " privileged to be present." The number of patients in a leper home did not simply increase : " she had the joy of seeing her afflicted flock increase from sixty-six to eighty-two." If those who used such language in sincerity stood in need of defence, it would be enough to say that they were in earnest about the things that are most worth caring about and that they were resolved to bring back the sense of God into every detail of their lives. But it was a mistake to " seek to wind themselves too high," to live at that extreme tension, with all the roots of action always set in the light of the conscious mind, as though

> " nothing of itself will come
> But we must still be seeking."

Yet if they had listened more closely to Jesus Himself, they might have been saved from that mistake and they would have been better interpreters of their Lord. For many have found that it is sufficient to change their whole view of religion when they surrender themselves to His free speech. One touch of His

F

gracious humour will relax that paralysing tension of mind which so often overtakes those who take religion most seriously.

The humour of Jesus constantly disconcerts the commentators. Consider His teaching about love in the cases where loving seems most difficult. He forbade retaliation when we are wronged and told us to love our enemies,—but not with a pained expression. His words are blithe and almost gay. " If a man smite thee on the one cheek "—a momentary pause while each man thought fiercely what was to be done in such a case,—but not one of them imagined *His* answer, which when it came took their breath away. It was as though He said, " Well, you have another." Now if any cares to stir the dust of old bookshelves and look up the commentators and homilists, he may see what a man looks like when he is *trying* to love his enemies but not to love them too much. Imagining that humour is something beneath the dignity of our Lord, and feeling bound to show cause, if at any point they cannot take His words quite literally, they take care to remind us that " Our Lord Himself when smitten by the servant of the High Priest, protested,"[1] that " from the ex-

[1] Ellicott.

amples which our Lord mentions, it is plain that this forbearance and compliance is required only when we are *slightly* attacked, but by no means when the assault is of a capital kind. In some cases smiting on the cheek, taking away one's coat, and compelling one to go a mile, may be great injuries and therefore ought to be resisted. But admitting that this rule has for its object small injuries, it is liable to no objection, for he who bears a slight affront, consults his honour and interests much better than he who resists or resents it."[1] And if a Christian decides, on the due occasion, but always making sure that it is the due occasion, not to prosecute a criminal, he is comforted in that difficult act of restraint by the reflection that " there are generally men of the world enough to deal with such depredators ; and a disciple of Christ seldom has occasion to waste his time or lose his temper about them."[2] And, finally, Doddridge completes the neutralising process in a smooth and many-syllabled paraphrase. " But I say unto you, that when you meet with ill-usage in the world, you do not immediately set yourselves against the injurious person in a posture of hostile opposi-

[1] Benson.　　　　[2] Thomas Scott.

tion, and with a resolution to return evil for evil; but where the damage is not great, choose rather to pass it by, though possibly it might on that account be repeated, than to enter into a rigorous prosecution of the offender. On these principles if any man strike thee on thy right cheek, *patiently* turn the other to him also." Observe how the pedestrian word, *patiently*, drains out the life and spirit of the passage, surrenders the initiative, and turns a blithe and active courage into a passive submission. Our author proceeds, " And if any one be resolved to sue thee at law and take away thy vest, permit him to take thy mantle also, for the loss of both would be but a trifle in comparison of those vexations, snares and expenses which would probably attend the continuance of the suit . . . for in many such cases as these, it will be more for your own comfort, as well as the credit of your profession, to submit than to contend."[1]

If we were doubtful of the place of humour in religion, futilities like these might convince us how disastrous is the want of it. For these same writers were not among the small fry of the well-meaning; they were great interpreters and could rise on occasion to the

[1] Doddridge, *Family Expositor*.

height of their theme and show the deep
things of God. But here they do nothing but
hide or weaken the truth which Jesus con-
veyed : and instances might be multiplied.
Jesus said, " When thou doest thine alms, do
not sound a trumpet before thee." It is surely
plain enough what he meant ; and if humour
had not been inhibited, so great a scholar as
Lightfoot would not have needed to say, " I
have not found, although I have sought for it
much and seriously, even the least mention of a
trumpet in almsgiving " ; nor would Morison
have needed to reply that "he need not have
sought so diligently, for we may be sure that in
the synagogues literal trumpets could not have
been employed when *private* individuals were
wishing to give charity." Other writers were
less scrupulous, however, than Lightfoot, or perhaps were more in love with " literal trumpets,"
for they say " In the East, it was the custom
to sound a trumpet before giving alms, on
pretence of calling the recipients together."

If humour is the perceiving of unexpected
resemblances or unexpected incongruities
whose discovery occasions surprise and delight
to the hearer, one need not seek long for it in
the teaching of Jesus. When they found fault
with Him because His followers were not fast-

ing when others were, He answered that you cannot patch old clothes with new cloth ; the more you patch, the worse they tear. We do not wonder that His critics did not know how to continue the argument ; but was ever so great a revolution announced in so homely a figure, for it declared that Judaism was outworn and that He had come to replace it with something new ? When He wanted to expose our passion for correcting other people's faults by way of distracting attention from our own, He chose to put it this way : " How can you say to your brother, ' Let me take out the splinter from your eye,' when there lies the plank in your own eye ? " The picture is grotesque but it is unforgettable and every man of honest mind turns the ridicule upon himself. Jesus does not use abstract terms about the futility of anxiety but He asks whether by worrying we can add a cubit to our stature (a notion which if we thought about it at all would make us smile) and then adds, " If you cannot manage a trifle like that, what is the use of troubling about things that are really difficult." He observed that the Pharisees were satisfied neither with the asceticism of John the Baptist nor with His own freedom. But no one but Jesus would have ventured so daring a figure as to liken them to children who would neither play at weddings nor funerals, with a hint that they might think of John as inviting them to play at funerals while He played the wedding game. He is, indeed, never at pains to make His sayings foolproof, but assumed that His hearers will not be wooden-minded. When we are slighted, however, most of us do know how to add a cubit to our stature, and therefore we understand the frame of mind in which Simon Peter came to Him with a strained face to ask how many times he was to forgive a brother, wondering how long this difficult business of forgiving was to go on and when he is to be free to say " That's the last." " Is it seven times ? " he asked. Was there no accompanying smile, when Jesus picked up the word " seven " and answered " Seventy times seven." If this were uttered with " the calm solemnity " of which we have heard, I should have reckoned that He meant four hundred and ninety. Uttered as it was, we catch a glimpse for a moment, of a nature too happy to take offence, too royal to retaliate, too much in love with loving to surrender the last chance of a reconciliation. If we see this, we see something of what Jesus meant.

There are three parables of Jesus where one would have thought the humour was undeniable. The first is the story of the labourers in the vineyard which is given with greater wealth of dramatic detail than most of the parables. We are able to watch those whole-day workmen at the end of the queue instinctively raising their claims when they see their Master's generosity to the late comers. " They supposed that they would get more, but they also got the penny they had agreed on." Then their complainings, " You have made these one-hour men equal to us!" Can anyone bring a fresh mind to such a scene without a smile, but a smile of compunction and self-blame.

In the other two parables, Jesus is asking us to consider how men behave when they are really in earnest about anything, in order that we may ask ourselves whether that is how we behave in spiritual concerns which we profess to take to God. A friend knocks up his neighbour in the night and asks for some food so that he may show hospitality to a traveller friend who has arrived unexpectedly. Since this is a parable about prayer, we should have expected a gracious answer. But what we hear is the voice of a man half asleep declaring that the door is shut (which is evi-

dent) and that the family has gone to bed and
that he cannot get up and give him bread at
this time. Give such a man a minute more
and he will be fast asleep again. But Jesus
proceeds, " Though he will not rise and give
for friendship's sake, yet because the man
kept on, he will in the end get up and give him
what he wants," plainly because it is less
trouble to rise up and be done with him rather
than have him shouting outside there all the
night. We have really no choice with a
passage like this : the story is wooden if it
is not humorous. And the same may be said
of the parallel story of the poor widow and
the unscrupulous judge.

It will not be supposed that what we are
arguing for is a pleasant turn here, a playful
word, a smiling simile there, in the teaching
of Jesus. We are concerned with something
much more pervasive and significant for the
understanding of Jesus, or of His religion. To
live without humour is to pass through life
wearing blinkers. If our one peril is distraction
from the business of the soul, if a rigorous
concentration is the chief of all virtues, if we are
intended to see only the road before us, and
not the country we are passing through,
humour is not an aid to religion. But of all the

diseases of religion, next to sheer slackness, perhaps the most common is a kind of mental cramp. It comes from the effort, often unconscious, to hold the mind continuously in a fixed posture, such as religion is supposed to require. There have been times in the past when men's environment was so corrupt that they were obliged, if they would be Christian, to walk as on hostile ground and always stand on the defensive against their surroundings. Part of the apparatus of defence was a special vocabulary of edification, a language which is at once a code among the initiated and a testimony to the outsider. But it was not God's will that religion should always mean this attitude of strained vigilance, and it was not the way of Jesus. The speech of Jesus could be passionate, austere, majestic; but it could pass to a lower tension and become familiar, homely, moving without fear among common things and borrowing from them all. There is an ease and sweetness in His handling of heavenly truth which comes as sudden relief to the mind and sets us wondering why we did not see it long ago. "Here is all friendliness and joy," and Jesus Himself is both utterly beyond us and yet the most knowable Person in the world.

Chapter IV

JESUS INTEGRATING LIFE

It is the business of religion to explain this life as well as to reveal another. We cannot offer any Christian or, indeed, any intelligible account of this life unless we can speak of another. During the last half-century there have been spiritual gains and losses, both of immense moment, but among the losses there has been none more serious than the decline in the sense of the eternal, not only among religious people, but among those who have little or no conscious religion at all. "The spiritual world, whether in Nature, in Art, or in definite religion, has vanished, and the curtain of the horizon has descended round the material things and the pitiful duration of human life. In former time in England, for better or worse, the things of the earth were shot with spiritual significance; heaven and hell stretched out as permanent realities; the 'kingdom of all the worlds' rose up as 'the theatre of man's achievements' and the 'measure of his destiny.' To-day amongst the masses of our great towns God is faintly apprehended as an amiable but absentee ruler; heaven and hell are passing to the memories of a far-off childhood, the one ceasing to attract, the other to alarm."[1] These words were written in 1902. But it cannot, I think, be contended that they are less true now. Our own generation is more effectually enclosed in the "nearest-at-hand" world; the curtains are more solid and the sense of any eternal significance in human life has fallen by many degrees.

The witness of the Church has failed seriously at this point. Hell disappeared fifty years ago, and heaven faded ten years later; and as the suspicion of some such change spread uneasily over Christian people, the pulpits went silent about the Hereafter. It was indeed very difficult for them to speak. Great questions had to be rethought. It was not possible to repeat the old threatenings; but neither was it possible to make fresh affirmations without first offering some retractations; and this meant controversy and the loss which controversy involves. Meanwhile there were other themes on which it seemed

[1] C. F. G. Masterman in *The Heart of the Empire*, p. 9.

more to the purpose to dwell. The world was changing fast. The little self-contained communities of olden time were everywhere disappearing, and the modern world had arrived in their place, offering to men a far more crowded programme of life, with greater prizes and sharper penalties and a crop of problems unknown before. Life here and now seemed interesting enough, or difficult enough, as the case might be, to absorb all the energies of man.

The Christian Church could not ignore these changes, but it ought not to have surrendered its witness to the eternal, which was never more needed than then. Whatever could be done to vindicate the Christian religion within the bounds of this present life, even if there is no other, has been done during this generation, and it has had its small successes. But the full result of this evacuation of the soul's native country has been disastrous. The attempt was indeed from the beginning intellectually absurd. Christianity offers itself as a religion of infinite dimensions. Its moments are the Divine Incarnation, the Cross and the Resurrection ; and these are conceivable and proportionable to the end in view, if this life is in fact the " vale of soul-making," the school for an endless life. But if, at the best, we are only cattle of a superior breed, the history of the Christian Faith is just a chapter in mythology. If there is any process of moral and spiritual education going on within us, such as gives value to every human personality, it is evident not only that the process is unfinished with any one of us when death comes, but also that it should never have been begun, if it was destined there to end. The " rationalist " who holds that the human personality has no better claim to survival than dogs or apes is logical in refusing to tolerate religion even as a hobby, for on his hypothesis it is a mischievous nuisance, diverting people from their true task of making the best of the only world there is. I cannot believe that the Christian Church can continue to leave the after-life postulated as a mere unknown ; and although our fathers proclaimed a Heaven and Hell in forms now incredible to us, our prudent silence is a poor substitute for their vehement and effective witness.

But religion must explain this life as well as reveal another, and our present failure to make things unseen and eternal vivid and potent to the mind of our age, is partly explained as a reaction from a mistaken kind of other-worldliness which dismissed this present world too summarily and under inadequate categories. All religion, in so far as it persuades of things eternal, must run the risk of lessening the significance of things temporal. But evangelical religion, that is to say the Christian religion, runs a special risk because, with its offer of the free grace of God, in which all good things are given, it must warn us against any dependence on conduct or " good works," or any notion of deserving what is given. If sincerity declines, then *corruptio optimi pessima;* the schism between the here and the hereafter becomes more abrupt, and when the degenerating process is complete, Heaven is secured by faith and forgiveness, and this is religion. Self-interest may then take charge of the present life.

There is, of course, no truth that cannot be corrupted and there is no way of guaranteeing sincerity in the handling of religion; but men might have been better guarded against this disintegration of their moral universe if religion had not been presented to them so vividly as a way of escape and so faintly as a motive to character. Theology, endeavouring to systematise the Christian thought of God and divine things, took shape as a theology of escape. No doubt this is one aspect of the

Christian religion, but it is not the only one nor the noblest, and it ought not to have become the formative element in theology. Certainly it brought home to men the urgency of the great issue, but it recognised only one point of departure for a religious life, and Bunyan has furnished the classical description :

" I dreamed and behold I saw a man clothed with rags, standing in a certain place, with his face from his own house, a book in his hand, and a great burden upon his back. I looked and saw him open the book and read therein ; and as he read, he wept and trembled ; and not being able longer to contain, he brake out with a lamentable cry, saying ' What shall I do ? ' "

We have travelled so far from the poignancy and truth of an experience like this, and have found so little satisfaction in the various forms of " religion without tears " which have supplanted it, that one hardly cares to offer criticism. But it is true that our fathers were at a loss to help anyone religiously, unless they could first bring him to this " deep sense of his sin and misery," or at least, an acute sense of his danger. This, to say truth, they rarely failed to do when the threat of eternal loss was so near and so unquestioned. There must have been many who went through some such expe-

rience as Bunyan describes when he went to
the bell-ringing.

" Before this, I had taken much delight in
ringing, but my conscience beginning to be
tender, I thought such practice was but vain
and therefore forced myself to leave it; yet my
mind hankered; wherefore I must go to the
steeple-house and look on, though I durst not
ring : but I thought this did not become religion neither; yet I forced myself and would
look on still, but quickly after, I began to think
how if one of the bells should fall ? Then I
chose to stand under a main beam that lay
overthwart the steeple, from side to side,
thinking here I might stand sure; but then I
thought again should the bell fall with a swing,
it might first hit the wall, and then, rebounding
upon me, might kill me for all this beam; this
made me stand in the steeple door : and now
thought I, I am safe enough; for if the bell
should now fall, I can slip out behind these
thick walls, and so be preserved notwithstand-
ing. So after this, I would yet go to see them
ring, but would not go any farther than the
steeple door; but then it came into my head,
how if the steeple itself should fall ? And this
thought ('it may, for aught I know, when I
stand and look on') did continually so shake

G

my mind, that I durst not stand at the steeple door any longer, but was forced to flee, for fear the steeple should fall upon my head."

Here is the urgency, beyond doubt, but as we can see, at a price. It was well to press the infinite significance of eternity, but if we treat this present life as trivial because it is transient, if we make a schism between things temporal and things eternal, so that they have no other relation than that of opposition, sooner or later the present world will assert its power and take its revenge. For the task of integration cannot in the end be evaded. However a man's mind may be set upon the Celestial City he has meanwhile to live in this present world, to eat and drink, to earn his daily bread, and mix with his fellows. And if he believes in God, and therefore in a universe and not a multiverse, he must believe that this present life is not meaningless, but has some relevance to the purpose of God. Heroic minds chose the ascetic solution. Man was placed here for his discipline in a hostile environment. He was to prove himself in conflict, and his wisdom was to have no unnecessary traffic with this world, to ask as little from it as he could, and to keep himself unentangled and unspotted by its manifold seductions.

If, however, the world was made so interesting as it is, only in order to provide occasions of temptation, and thereby exercise the
soul in conflict, it might perhaps be fair to
inquire whether the business of providing
temptation has not been a good deal overdone.
Since few of us in our day, however, are
tempted to follow the ascetic in his steep and
thorny path, we need not stay to press the
question. We are in much greater danger from
a certain weak compromise which has a far
wider vogue and is the more entangling because it is seldom articulated. The world may
be regarded as not so much hostile as neutral—a
region in which God is not much interested and
in which it is well if a Christian is not too much
interested either. Hence in these neutral
tracts of the common life, a Christian will
please God chiefly by his refrainings. He must
eat and drink—but religion intervenes with
the counsel not to enjoy it too much. He may
get gain—but not too much, nor get it unjustly
of course. He must sleep—but the saints retire
late and reluctantly, and rise early and
earnestly.

Jeremy Taylor, in his *Holy Living*, making
a plea for more time to be spent with God in
prayer and meditation, laments the time we

must spend " in eating and drinking, in necessary business and unnecessary vanities, in
worldly civilities and less useful circumstances
in the learning arts and sciences, languages or
trades," so that little time at the best is left
for " the practices of piety and religious walk-
ing with God," " for God and God's service."
The error here—for error it seems to me to be—
is only partly retrieved by the reflection that
God in His goodness " hath not only permitted
us to serve the necessities of our nature, but
hath made them to become parts of our duty ;
that if we by directing these actions to the
glory of God intend them as instruments to
continue our persons in His service, He by
adopting them into religion may turn our
nature into grace, and accept our natural
actions as actions of religion." There was, of
course, a noble motive behind the high tension
of such language. Their discipline was better
than our slackness. But the whole truth was
not there while the antithesis remained between
"serving God" and the "necessary serving of
ourselves," between " natural actions " and
" actions of religion," between " nature " and
" grace." We are not helped to see that the
appointments of this earthly life—day and
night, work and rest, hunger and food, adven-

ture and monotony, hazard and safety, are of God and therefore are of love, and have friendly significance in themselves. We are still left with two worlds, not one; and though we are told that all our doing may be done to the glory of God, it is rather as the mastery of an unfavourable environment, and the pressing of an alien thing into the service of God than as the realisation of a purpose of God planted even in the routine of everyday life. In spite of its better thoughts, the Christian Church has always had a sacred and a secular, for there were always tracts of human life in which it was not interested and others of which it was afraid. Sometimes it has called men out of their secular employment in order to find God. More often it has accepted the common life as inevitable, and urged men to discharge their part in it faithfully, but rather so as to be done with it than as rejoicing in it and looking to find a meaning of God in every part of it.

So someone has said : " If I am in the cotton business and feel the zest of it, does God feel any interest like my own ? If I struggle with my picture and at last get my bit of cloud just right, does God care about that too ? I enjoy *Punch* and *Pickwick*. Does God allow me to read them only as a sort of concession to my foolishness ? If I mind a machine all day, does God care about my bit of skill, my accuracy and deftness ? If I make buttons, does God care about buttons ? If the little boys play football, does God only say, " Little things please little minds " ? We can all give the right answers to such questions—when we remember. But when the catechism is over and we are off guard, the contrary habit of mind continually asserts itself, and we are seen moving uneasily to and fro between the real world where God is, and that No Man's Land where all divine significances wither and die.

But we have not so learned Christ if we have been content to be taught by His ways on earth. *His* life, at any rate, was one whole. His mind, like His robe, was " without seam, woven from the top throughout." Wherever He looked, in the world of nature or the world of men, He saw purpose and meaning, and Someone who meant it. Everywhere He saw God, but always God working—not looking on. The visible world was for Him a

> " mighty sum
> Of things for ever speaking."

For Him, the heavens were always declaring the glory of God and the firmament showing

His handiwork. The generation to which Jesus
spoke was not quick to catch the poetry of His
references to the beauty and meaning of creation. Apart from His words there are hardly
any parallels in the New Testament to the
Nature poetry of some Old Testament passages. But the few words of His which they
have preserved must surely be the survivors of
many other sayings which fell on unprepared
minds and were soon forgotten. What was recorded is beyond price. The sun rising on the
evil and the good, the rain falling on the just
and the unjust, were, to the mind of Jesus, the
sacraments of a divine love that was far too
deep to stoop to reprisals or to be turned back
from its poignant quest by any repulses. He
saw birds flying without care and flowers
beautiful without toil, but these, too, had a
meaning beyond themselves. God's handiwork
was visible upon them and they also were the
sacraments of an unfailing care which it is our
misery that we cannot trust. Jesus heard men
on all hands trying to patch up their credit and
swearing by this and that to get themselves
believed. There may be fifty ways of rebuking
such a habit. His way was to tell us that there
is nothing to swear by that is not God's. The
Heavens are God's throne ; the earth His foot-

stool ; Jerusalem his city. Even a man's head is not his own ; he cannot make one hair white or black. There is not a spot which is not holy ground. Sun and stars, wind and rain, birds and flowers—the whole universe is one vast embassy to God's estranged children and all the ambassadors are saying, " Be ye reconciled to God." The visible world and the invisible are no longer two, but one in the Father's love for His children.

To assent to this as truth is nothing. To receive it and live by it is to be new created and to find all things made new. For at any time, the wonder of a sunrise, the quiet of evening, one single star, the sound of falling rain, the breath of a cool wind, the stillness of a tree— any one of a thousand things may pass the secret signal to the waiting mind, open the heavens and fill the blank world with the presence of the Friend. And when the doubt returns, whether this is not all " subjectivism," whether we are not merely endowing inanimate Nature with a soul, for our own comfort, and finding no other God than that which our minds had first created, nothing answers that doubt more effectually than the remembrance of Him who, with steadier vision than we can conceive, saw the Father " always working," making the sun to rise on the evil as well as on the good because that was His way of loving His enemies.

The world of men also was God's world to the mind of Jesus. It is clear that He took delight in all the healthful instincts and activities of the human family. He was glad to be among men and was not impatient to go. He speaks of the deep things of God and of ourselves, but these things do not lie apart from the working life of men. Common objects, daily concerns, ordinary persons behaving like ordinary persons, run into His speech, to show His meaning and to receive in return new meaning themselves. It seems as though His eyes missed nothing and His hospitable heart refused nothing that was human. In particular the labour of men had an inexhaustible interest for Him. The whole busy life of His time is present to His mind because it was dear to His heart—father and son, mother and child, landlord and tenant, employer and employed, soldiers and sailors, shepherds, farmers, gardeners, merchants, builders, bankers, bakers, all these are there and all of them about their business, moving, acting, changing things about them. There are no lay figures. If Jesus speaks of farming, He does not as an outsider will do, picture the farmer in contemplative mood, watching his crops grow on quiet summer evenings. He shows him at his labour, persevering in spite of discouragements, seeing much of his sowing wasted, but rewarded in the end by the hard-won harvest. If he speaks of a shepherd it is not in the soothing strains of pastoral music, nor does He make us think of innocent sheep cropping innocent grass on starlit nights. He describes the shepherd out on his hardest and most dangerous work, refusing to be daunted or to despair, and bringing back his one lost sheep at last. No wonder that the shepherd, as he listened, felt that Jesus understood him better than he understood himself, and that the sower asked " Has he been sowing too ?" The woman went back to her patching and her baking, the steward to make up his accounts, and the fisherman to let down his nets, each of them with a better heart because His eye had lingered upon them and His mind had given them a place. He never spoke as though our daily work were a punishment imposed, as the writer of Genesis does, nor as a futility, as the Preacher in Ecclesiastes and some others do. Daily work and Sabbath worship were not two, but one, in the Father's purpose. He brought to light the world of unseen things and stirred men with aspirations which astonished themselves, but He never put a man out of love with life or left him resentful of its common tasks.

He was for a great part of His public ministry a homeless man, and He knew how to take things as they came without complaint. But He remained sensitive to the sufferings of others and felt the hardships of human life. His ministry of healing shows how He felt about bodily pain and weakness. The thought of hungry men distressed Him and He would not send them empty away. "When He saw the crowds, He was moved with compassion." His ear caught the grinding of that interior friction of mishandled lives, which wears away the strength of men, and leaves them fear-haunted, spent, overstrained and unhappy— when it might be all otherwise if they would. From that compassionate insight came the invitation with the amazing claim which it involves : " Come unto Me, all ye that labour and are heavy laden, and I will give you rest. Take my yoke upon you and learn of me ; for I am meek and lowly in heart : and ye shall find rest unto your souls. *For my yoke is easy and my burden is light.*" Not one of the apostles would have denied that last word, but not one of them would have thought of saying it.

It does not need to be said that Jesus well knew the evil that was in the world and understood how far were our ways from what God intended them to be. There are many words of His all aflame with moral passion, which once heard can never be forgotten. " If thy hand offend thee, cut it off. If thine eye offend thee, pluck it out. Better go into life maimed than go with all your powers into hell." " Whosoever shall cause one of these little ones which believe on me to stumble, it were better for him if a great millstone were hanged about his neck, and he were cast into the sea." We understand why the seer of Patmos said that a sharp two-edged sword went out of His mouth. Yet even in dealing with moral evil His ways are not what we should have expected. The ease of His behaviour among morally disreputable people startles us still. We wonder that He did not recoil from their coarse contamination, and that they did not recoil from His purity. The intellectual distance which separated Him from those with whom He mixed was immeasurable and the moral distances were still more hopeless. Yet He contrived the way, the miracle happened and He and they drew near. The sinless One came nearer to these sinners than they could come to each other. His sympathy with them was unforced, natural and deep. He was patient with them, but not with the patience which concludes by saying, " I have listened patiently to all you say." He went to the houses of unpleasant people and sat down to meat with them, glad to be there and making others glad to have Him. And when He left it was with pressing invitations to come again. It must have seemed sometimes as though He had forgotten to do them good. We might have imagined that being what He was, His mere entrance into such a company would have brought all ordinary intercourse to a stand in one tremendous moral challenge. But it is plain that this was not usually the case. There would have been no point in the frequent taunts of the Pharisees about the company that He kept, if the entrance of Jesus had always been the signal for a moral crisis in which men were driven forthwith to repudiate Him or to repent and amend their lives. He was not disconcerted, as many of us would have been to find bad people more cheerful than they had a right to be. He knew when to be urgent and peremptory and He knew when to refrain and try another way. He knew how to be at home with sinners without condoning sin. He could offer friendship to those who were unworthy of it, and His friendship was as untainted by compromise as by condescension.

One may look at Jesus as He is shown to us in the Gospels for twenty years and still be overtaken by fresh wonder. " The latchet of His shoes we are not worthy to unloose." His heart was the home of every beatitude and a harmony of whatsoever things are true, honourable, pure, lovely and of good report. Three years of crowded toil—of unbroken peace. Preaching, teaching, healing, and all at a speed which left His companions breathless—but all unhurried. He spoiled none of His gifts by haste, could wait as well as work, did nothing before the time, rose early to pray, gave nights to communion with God and found leisure to talk with a derelict woman by the well and to watch children at their play. He knew how to be alone, but He was not a recluse. The Man of Sorrows and not less the Man of Joys : serious but not strained, His humour without levity, utterly kind and utterly inexorable, tolerant and uncompromising, full of grace and truth. But no! We cannot describe Him. He is wider and greater than we know and even when we mean to praise Him, we distort the fair image of His mind and do Him wrong. Yet being what He was and is, He would not, we think, be displeased if to some of us He seems to be the most knowable Person in the world, and His human face the perfect revelation of the glory of God.